Deep Routes

Deep Routes

by
Dr. Cody W. Moree

Bladensburg, MD

Deep Routes

Published by Inscrript Books
A Division of Dove Christian Publishers
P.O. Box 611
Bladensburg, MD 20710-0611

www.dovechristianpublishers.com

Copyright © 2020 by Dr. Cody W. Moree

Cover Design by Mark Yearnings

Library of Congress Control Number: 2020938606

ISBN: 978-1-7348625-1-5 (paperback)

First Edition

Printed in the United States of America

This book is dedicated to the man who raised me as his son, even though he did not have to—my Dad, Coach Harold Hill.

Coach Hill was my first example of how football should be more than just a game, and how faith in Jesus should be a part of football.

Introduction

I've often said that I've learned the essential things in life on the football field. I think it may be because football mimics life with incredible accuracy. In football and in life, we are given a finite amount of time to fulfill our purpose. In both arenas, we quickly learn that we need others to accomplish our goals, and that which we do with those closest to us brings the most satisfaction.

Both football and life require a distinct relationship between the player and the Head Coach. The player must demonstrate unwavering trust and commitment. He must have the constant knowledge that the Head Coach has a genuine desire to see the player succeed.

In the Old Testament book of Jeremiah, the ultimate Head Coach, our Heavenly Father, says, "*'I know the plans I have for you,' declares the Lord, 'plans to bless you, not to harm you, plans to give you hope and a future'" (Jer. 29.11).* The Head Coach is reminding us that He has crafted a specific and personal game plan for each of us, and if we follow it, we will win!

We all want to win, but anyone remotely familiar with athletics knows that winning, especially winning consistently, is not easy. It's not supposed to be easy, but it is the goal, both on the football field and in the Christian life. To strive for anything else is just wrong. The Apostle Paul writes, "*We run to **win** the race!*"

In Corinthians 15:57, Paul also reminds us that *Victory* is the gift to every Christian. It was a hard-fought win with a tremendous price but is ours. We do not win because of our own talents and abilities, but because Jesus secured eternal victory with His death and resurrection.

Well, if that's the case, why is victory so hard to find, and, if we do happen to stumble across it, why is it so difficult to grasp? Why do so many born-again believers live like the other team just ran up the score on them rather than the champions which Jesus worked so hard for us to become?

One reason might be that the concept of winning is often misunderstood. Some equate winning with always getting what we want, having a stress-free existence, or being comfortable. As a football coach, I can assure you those are not elements associated with a championship-caliber football team. Football is seldom stress-free and hardly ever comfortable. Football can be painful, disappointing, and exhausting – but for those of us who really love it, it's worth every minute.

The life of the Christian is no different. It can be riddled with heartache, disappointment, and pain, but for those of us who love Jesus, it's worth every minute. Why? Because our Head Coach loves us more than his own life, and He wants us to win!

He wants us to have real victory, not some temporary emotional rush that fades once the moment has passed. He wants us to live a championship life.

How we do that? That's what *Deep Routes* is all about. In the next few pages, we will look at a few football situations and how they relate to real life. The way we handle each of them can determine if we have authentic victory or if we are merely trying to exist on the unreliable emotion of situational happiness.

Whether you are a coach, an athlete, a fan, or a friend or relative of someone who is, this book is for you.

In football and in life, there comes a time when we are no longer content with short gains. At some point, you have to stretch the defense and go deep. This book is designed to help you stretch and grow as a Christian.

Get ready. Let's go deep!

Day 1

Self-Acceptance

He had no beauty or majesty to attract us to him, nothing in his appearance that we should desire him. He was despised and rejected by men, a man of sorrows and familiar with suffering. Like one from whom men hide their faces, he was despised and we esteemed him not. Surely he took up our infirmities and carried our sorrows, yet we considered him stricken before God, smitten by him, and afflicted. But he was pierced for our transgressions, he was crushed for our iniquities. The punishment that brought us peace was upon him and by his wounds we are healed.

(Isaiah 53:2b-5)

We're Not All Quarterbacks

I've been coaching public school football for a long time now. A lot has changed over the years, but there's one aspect of coaching at this level that will probably never change. Most kids begin their public school football career in the seventh grade. It's so funny because most of them know little, if anything, about organized football. Still, I've seldom met an incoming seventh-grader who didn't want to be the quarterback. Better still, I've rarely met a seventh grader's mom who didn't think her son should *get* to be the quarterback.

In reality, very few athletes want to play quarterback once they realize the demands of the position. Initially, the QB appears to be the glamorous one on the team. He gets all the attention. He's in the spotlight. He's usually the good-looking one on the team, and if we're honest, that all sounds pretty good.

I have come to a stark realization. I don't look like me anymore. I remember *the me* of a couple of decades ago, and I look nothing like him. The former *me* was not a bad looking guy, as looks go. He was tall, thin, tan, and toned. And, oh man, did he have hair!

The old me was a product of the 1980s. Big hair was an absolute requirement. The old me wore only the latest, most popular clothes, and he very seldom wore them twice. The old me was exactly what society said he should be. I was the guy who wanted to be the quarterback, not because I should be, but because it looked cool.

Now when I look in the mirror, my former self is nowhere to be found. And I realize that is a good thing. Along with my big hair came big problems. Arrogance, vanity, and selfishness were some of my better qualities. I was extremely unapproachable. After all, if I allowed someone to get too close, they might mess up my hair! I wish I were joking, but sadly that was the truth. The most troubling aspect of this time in my life was the constant stress and fear of trying to maintain this false image and keeping anyone from finding out how insecure I was.

Not being comfortable in your own skin will absolutely rob you of your joy. In a futile effort to be something we are not, the façade we construct becomes a wall that prevents others from experiencing who we really are. This is a game we can never win.

It is not only our appearance to which we apply makeup and hairspray. We try to dress up our marriages, jobs, relationships, and just about everything else in our lives that we think doesn't look just right. We sure don't get this play from our Head Coach.

The book of Isaiah describes what Jesus looked like as an adult man. *"He had no beauty or majesty. Nothing about Him was attractive. Nothing in His appearance was desirable"* (53:2).

Unlike us, Jesus could look any way He wanted. He could have had movie-star looks, but He knew there was no victory in that. He knew that winning takes place much deeper within us, and it's only when we remove the outer layers that we find the end zone.

Day 2

Perspective

*Now we see but a poor reflection as in a mirror; then we
shall see face to face. Now I know in part; then I shall
know fully, even as I am fully known.*

(1 Corinthians 13:12)

Painting the Football Field

There are two types of people in the world. That's it. It seems
like there should be dozens, if not hundreds, of types, but when
we remove all the tags and labels of society, it becomes evident
that everyone fits in one of only two categories: those who can't
believe just how bad their lives are, and those who can't believe
just how great their lives are. Ironically, the circumstances in
both cases are often similar if not identical.

In my initial year as a high school football coach, I first experi-
enced the extra duties associated with this profession. To this day,
I remember vividly walking behind a paint machine on a hot August afternoon in Haskell, Texas. I recall saying to myself, "I can't
believe I *get* to do this." I was a very happy twenty-one year old
because painting the field was a part of coaching football.

A few years ago, I was marking and painting the football
field in Apple Springs, Texas, where I currently serve as the
superintendent and head football coach. We were getting ready
for the start of two-a-days.[1] I remember vividly saying to my-

---

1 When a team goes through two trainings on the same day.

self (and probably anyone else within earshot), "I can't believe I *have* to do this." I was a very unhappy fifty-one-year-old because painting the field was a part of coaching football.

There was little or no difference between the details in those two scenarios. August is hot and painting is painting. In reality, painting the field did not make me happy or unhappy. Aerosol paint cans can't do that. It was me and the two distinctly different ways I chose to view the very same task that determined my attitude.

Here's the crazy thing about perspective. The default setting is always on negative. We don't have to work to see bad in people or in circumstances. If we do nothing, we get an automatic and constant flow of negativity. But, if we want to live a life of genuine victory and contentment, effort is required. We must make the conscious decision to override the default setting and literally flip the switch. We must determine to play the game of life from a position of blessing.

Day 3

Forget the Past

He has removed our sins as far from us as the east is from the west.

(Psalm 103:12 NLT)

Glory Days

I've noticed a trend lately. The older I get, the better athlete I used to be! I remembered being a decent player in my 20s and 30s. By my 40s, I was downright awesome. Now I look back at my playing days and wonder how anyone could have been as good as I was. By the time I am 65 or 70, I am sure that I will be telling people that I won the Super Bowl as a senior in high school.

The same thing happens to me when I go fishing. The farther I get from the lake, the bigger that fish becomes. The past has a wonderful ability that allows us to remember things the way we want to and not always the way they actually were. That's not altogether bad as long as we know we are just having fun. The danger comes when we romanticize the past so much that we can't enjoy the present.

If we long for the good old days to the point where we can't live in the moment, it will rob us of the victory that was meant especially for today.

The opposite side of the coin can be more dangerous and destructive. All of us have had hurts in our past. It may be loss, pain inflicted by someone else, or even a critical error in judgment that we made ourselves and still causes us shame and embarrassment.

Regardless of the source, it was not a pleasant time, and we just can't seem to get over it. The clinical term for this feeling is 'arrested development.' The pain of the past literally stops us from moving forward, and it completely kills our joy. It will keep us from winning!

Arrested development does not have to continue. There is a cure. The Psalmist wrote, *"God's mercies are new every morning!"* This means that every day, our Maker gives us a brand-new, clean slate. God does not want us to play yesterday's game over again.

Today is a brand-new kick-off!

Day 4

Companions

As iron sharpens iron, so one man sharpens another.

(Proverbs 27:17)

Huddle Up

I love big cats. Always have. I'm not sure why, but I love big cats. For my 50ᵗʰ birthday, my family took me to a big cat sanctuary where I got to hold and play with lion cubs and tiger cubs. Even though my birthday fell during the heart of football season, we went anyway! I'll confess that I tried to sneak a baby lion out of there, but my wife made me give him back.

Lions and tigers share many common characteristics. Both species are strong, powerful, carnivores at the top of their respective food chains. There is one stark difference between these two majestic animals. Lions are communal. They live in prides. Tigers are solitary creatures. They spend most of their adult lives completely alone.

In this respect, our DNA is more like a lion than the tiger. We are not solitary beings. We live, work, and play with many other people. This was the plan from the beginning. The first time in recorded history, where God determines that something is not complete, happens early in the book of Genesis. In the book's second chapter, God declared that it is not good for man to be alone.

In football and in life, victory is directly related to the relationships we have with the other people who share our huddle. The friends and companions we choose will either strengthen or weaken us. So, we must be sure to fill our huddle with those who influence us positively, demand the best from us, and help us to become the greatest version of ourselves.

No one, regardless of their personal talent, wins a football game alone. One of the first things we learn from football is the absolute necessity for strong and courageous teammates. We have to be able to look in the eyes of our teammates and know that when we break the huddle and head to the line of scrimmage, we are all determined to win.

Relationships that are always draining, stressful, negative, and toxic will deplete us of our energy and rob us of our joy. We actually learn to *"play down"* to lower expectations. Such relationships will ultimately cost us the game.

Lions understand the concept of the huddle very well. If they associate with the hyena, they have an adversarial relationship. They must always be on guard. They must always watch their backs. They must sleep with one eye open. The hyena may appear to be helping the lion, but in reality, it is always looking for a way to help itself, even to the detriment of the lion. But if the lion forms a strong pride with others who are like-minded and dedicated to the success of the group, then everyone eats well, everyone is content, everyone is happy.

A football team will typically huddle up before every play. It's important to gather with trusted teammates, especially before significant events and major decisions. We all need to be part of a strong pride. We need a pack, a posse, a huddle that will hold us accountable and enrich our lives.

Check your huddle and check it often. It should only contain those teammates given to us by the Head Coach Himself.

Day 5

Eliminate Worry

*Therefore I tell you, do not worry about your life…Who
of you by worrying can add a single hour to your life…
Do not worry about tomorrow for tomorrow will worry
about itself.*

(Matthew 6: 25-34a)

Just Play

One of the hallmarks of good coaching is the ability to instill confidence in the players. I suppose that's true at any level, but it is especially critical in high school football. The last thing I want my kids to do is overthink. I don't want them to worry about the limitless number of variables that could occur during any football play. Yes, I want them mentally prepared, and I want them to make good decisions. But, there comes a time when they must put all of that aside and just play.

When high school football players worry about what could go wrong, it usually does. So, my coaches and I must remind them often that things will be okay. The game will go on. The sun will rise the next morning. Don't worry, just play.

Think about the last time you were seriously worried about something. Got it? Now think about your life and how things turned out after that event or situation became history. No matter what it was, or how it turned out, you made it. You are still here.

How much good did it do you to worry about that particular time in your life? Did worrying change the outcome, good or bad, in any way? No, it did not. How do I know? I know because my name is Cody, and I am a worrier. Just as an alcoholic has to admit he or she has a problem, so did I.

I used to worry about everything. It was a way of life for me. I even used to worry that I was not concerned or troubled enough. Seriously, I used to worry about not worrying enough! I was a lot of fun back then.

One day I was listening to a message from the Sermon on the Mount. I was actually paying attention this particular day when our pastor read the words of Jesus as He said, *"do not worry."* It hit me. The very same God who said, *"do not steal"* and *"do not kill"* also said, *"do not worry."*

For the first time, I realized that worrying was actually a sin. It was really quite simple. Jesus said don't do it, and I did it – a lot! Therefore, I was deliberately disobedient.

Jesus not only said worry is wrong, but He also said it is a complete waste of time. He asked, *"Who among you can add even one hour to your life by worrying?"* The word translated into worry in the New Testament means 'to divide the mind.' I just can't afford that. If you divide my mind in half, there's not much left to work with!

Worry is a thief. It will rob you of your time, your energy, your relationships, your health, and especially your joy. Worry can't change your circumstances or what lies ahead. Don't waste your time on something with no pay-off. Invest your time into a relationship with the One who can change everything.

One of the many benefits of the Cross is that we no longer have to worry. Jesus made it possible for us to just play!

Day 6

No Fear

For God did not give us a spirit of timidity, but a spirt of power, of love and of self-discipline.

(2 Timothy 1:7 NLT)

Hit Somebody

Let's be honest. Football is a brutal game. We shouldn't be apologetic or evasive about that. Hard hits and violent collisions are part of the game. It was designed to be this way. This is one of the aspects of the sport that actually make it fun and make it a good illustration of life.

Of course, we never want to see someone injured on the football field.

Ironically, I have found that injury occurs more frequently when players are afraid of a potential injury. When one's underlying objective on the football field is to avoid injury, it changes the way they play the game. When a player is subconsciously motived by fear, it stifles all that he tries to do. Sure, he can go through the motions. He can look like a football player, but he's not really playing and, rest assured, he's not winning.

Fear and the memory of pain can be emotionally paralyzing. It will cause us to freeze in our tracks and not risk the next decision, relationship, opportunity, or adventure. In both life and football, this is when real injury usually occurs. To stand still, frozen in fear, on the football field is one of the most dangerous things a player can do. That's why we tell our kids to always be moving, don't just stand there, and, when in doubt, hit somebody!

Fear is a potent and crafty emotion. It can cloak itself in many forms. Bitterness, rudeness, anger, jealously, and reclusiveness are all just outward expressions of inner fears.

Unrealistic, unconquered fears will rob us of our joy, destroy our chance for victory, and often cause the very pain we are desperately trying to avoid.

And like weapons of war, fear will often cause collateral damage to those around us. It can cause us to inflict injury on our own teammates. It's hard to recognize, but our fear can actually steal the game away from those we love.

Unhealthy fear does not come from God. Scripture tells us that *"God does not give us a spirit of fear."* Instead, He is the solution. To gain access to that solution, we must do two things. First, we must acknowledge that we are powerless over our fears. Next, we must realize that God has complete and total power. If you will pardon my East Texas slang, He ain't scared of nothin'!

The game of life is too important to play from a position of fear. The sacrifice that Jesus made was far too expensive for us to stay bound to the sidelines by our fears. He does not want that for us, so please do not settle for it.

Day 7

Unity

Live in harmony with one another. If it is possible, as far as it depends on you, live at peace with everyone.

(Romans 12:16a, 18)

Team First

God bless Tony Romo!

Finally, we saw someone of national prominence put the interests of others above themselves. In case you missed it, the long-time starting quarterback of the Dallas Cowboys, Tony Romo, broke a bone in his back right before the start of the 2016 season. To everyone's amazement, rookie Dak Prescott stepped in and guided the Cowboys to their best performance in decades.

When Tony got well, he held a press conference and said, in part, "Dak Prescott deserves to be our quarterback. We have something special going on, and I will get out the way and support Dak and our team."

The truth is Tony Romo did not have to take this approach. Getting hurt was not his fault. He had done nothing wrong to lose his job. He had been going the extra mile for years, when the Cowboys were not so good, carrying the weight of the team on his shoulders, literally; his collar bone was broken twice! By all rights, he deserved to get his job back. He could have played the entitlement card, but he did not.

Tony Romo wields incredible clout within the Cowboys

organization. He is a close, personal friend with owner Jerry Jones and former Head Coach Jason Garrett. Romo, Garrett, and their wives were often photographed together in the Dallas society pages. Once, when the NCAA basketball championships were played at Cowboys Stadium, the television camera panned up to Jerry Jones' luxury skybox. Sitting in the box together were Jones, President Bush, President Clinton, and Tony Romo. Tony could have played the influence card, but he did not. Tony played the team card. And, it was evident that his heart was breaking even as he did it.

Early in his career, Romo made some big mistakes that cost the Cowboys several key games. You may remember the botched field goal snap or the horrible interceptions late in big games. It became known as "pulling a Romo." Now, pulling a Romo has a whole new meaning.

We will never be Tony Romo. Most of us will not hang out with billionaires and former Presidents. All of us will be on a team. We may refer to our teams as families, churches, and jobs, but they are still teams. There will be many times when you will feel your needs are not being met by the team. You will be tempted to put your wants and needs above that of your teammates. Don't do it. Pull a Romo.

At some point, you will have an opportunity to make a teammate look bad while making yourself look really good. You won't even have to work at it. All you will have to do is go along with the gossip of the day. You can be passive-aggressive and take down a co-worker or a family member without ever firing a shot. Don't do it. Pull a Romo.

Victory is never found amid disunity. Oh sure, there may be temporary euphoria, but it won't last. Real winning happens to those who take the high road. Life, people, and circumstances will try to convince you to take the shortcut. Don't do it. Pull a Romo!

Day 8

Eternal Salvation

For the wages of sin is death, but the gift of God is eternal life in Christ Jesus our Lord.

(Romans 6:23)

Post-Game Celebration

Of all the many outstanding football coaches the world has known, there is none I admire more than the great Tom Landry. He was the genius in the funny hat who stoically strolled the sidelines of Dallas for more than a quarter of a century. Along the way, he invented schemes and strategies that revolutionized the game of football. He won every award imaginable. His twenty consecutive winning seasons are still the most recorded by any head coach in NFL history.

Tom Landry was a man I longed to emulate. Not only was he a phenomenal coach, but he was also a remarkable human being with character above reproach. He had a relationship with Jesus about which he was bold and unashamed. Tom Landry not only did things well, he did things right.

So, as a young football fan and later a budding football coach, I began to study the life and career of Coach Landry. I knew his history, his statistics, his offenses, and his defenses. I even knew the size of his trademark fedora. There was not much I couldn't tell you about Thomas Wade Landry.

At one point early in my coaching career, I wrote Coach

Landry a letter, never really expecting it to make it to him, much less ever hear from him. He was kind enough to write me a very personal response. Today, that letter hangs in my office.

On February 12, 2000, Tom Landry died. A huge celebration of his life was held in Dallas. It was broadcast on television. Of course, I was glued to the TV. I watched as world-wide dignitaries and NFL legends eulogized him.

Sometimes, the stories they told were just slightly incorrect. Perhaps the date was wrong or the score of a particular game was misquoted. Being a scholar on all things Tom Landry, I said to myself, "Wow, I know more about Tom Landry than some of those people do." Yet they were invited to the celebration and I was not.

Then it hit me. Those people didn't merely know *about* Tom Landry; they *knew* Tom Landry. They were his children, his players, and his fellow coaches. They had a personal relationship with him, and that's what it took to be invited to the celebration.

Scripture promises that one day there will be another great celebration. This celebration will not be for a great man who has died – it will be for the Great I Am who has risen! Once again, a personal relationship is the requirement for an invitation.

Like my knowledge of Coach Landry, you can know everything one can possibly know *about* Jesus and still not know Him. And like my letter from Coach Landry, you have a personal letter from Jesus, The Holy Bible, and may be able to quote chapter and verse, but still not have a personal relationship with the Author.

Don't settle for just a cognitive understanding of Jesus. Don't base your eternity on the Biblical facts you can acquire. As good as that may be, it simply will not get you into Heaven.

I never had the opportunity to meet Coach Landry in person, but you can meet Jesus, right where you are, right now. Ask Him to come into your heart and become your Savior. He will do it.

Trust me. You do not want to miss the celebration that God has planned for us once this life is over!

Day 9

Giving Up Control

Nations are in uproar, kingdoms fall; He lifts up his voice, the earth melts. The Lord Almighty is with us; the God of Jacob is our fortress.

(Psalm 46:6-7)

Remote Control

Men are usually very simple creatures. We typically don't need many frills to enjoy a happy existence. There is, however, some glaring exceptions to this rule. Many of us need to watch football, and we must always possess an acute knowledge as to the whereabouts of the television remote. A lack of such knowledge, even for a few seconds, will send most men into a state of panic. I can empathize with such pain. One day it happened to me.

We live in a rural area, out of range of local stations, so our programming is supplied through a satellite provider. I've got 300 channels! Now, I only watch westerns and football, but I've got 300 channels! On top of that, my remote was amazing. You could program it to do anything! It would operate the doorbell and computer. Heck, you couldn't get ice out of the refrigerator without using my remote!

And then, one day, everything stopped. It was a tragic day right in the middle of the play-offs. My remote was gone. It was nowhere to be found, and I had to come to grips with the fact that I was no longer in charge.

As painful as that time was, I actually learned a pretty good lesson. Being in control is a false reality, at best. We equip ourselves with the gadgets and gizmos of this world, in addition to jobs, wealth, and social status. We line them up in a precise order and try to convince everyone, especially ourselves, that we've got it all under control. Then one day, one of those earthly gadgets gets lost in the sofa cushions of life, and our control turns to chaos.

The reason we run into such trouble trying to secure control over our lives is that we are simply not built for it.

The truth is we were not made to be in charge. That is a job specifically designed by God for one person: Jesus. He called Himself the Good Shepherd. Guess what? That makes us the sheep. It may not be a flattering analogy, but it's quite accurate. Let's face it. We really don't want sheep to be in charge of things.

As long as we struggle to gain control of our lives, we will forfeit our joy. Fortunately, the opposite is also true.

As soon as we relinquish control to Jesus, joy begins to replace the emptiness of superficial control. The Apostle Paul referred to it as "daily dying to self." How do we really do that? It begins when we tender our resignation.

As soon as we get up every morning, we must resign as the CEO of our world. We must consult the Lord on every decision, and acknowledge that He has the ability and the authority to call any play He deems best. He promises to replace our futile attempt at control with genuine contentment.

Oh, and by the way, I got a new TV remote. It cost $89.95. Actually, the remote itself was only $9.95, but it takes $80 bucks to have one of those things shipped overnight!

Day 10

Spiritual Flexibility

*For I know the plans I have for you declares the Lord,
plans to prosper you and not to harm you, plans to give
you hope and a future. (Jeremiah 29:11)*

Are You Coachable?

Rayfield Wright is considered to be one of the greatest Dallas Cowboys of all time. It didn't start out that way. Wright was drafted by the Cowboys to play tight end, the position he played in college—the position he loved. Unfortunately, his skills as a tight end were marginal at best by NFL standards. His head coach, the great Tom Landry, saw something in Wright that convinced him that Rayfield would be a much better offensive tackle. Coach Landry summoned Wright to his office and informed him that he would have to change positions.

Wright hated the idea. As a tight end, he would get to catch the ball. He would get to score touchdowns. At offensive tackle, he would never touch the football. Instead, his sole job would be to block for others who did. His own dreams would never come to pass. He told Coach Landry he did not want to change positions but reluctantly agreed to give it a try.

The rest was, as they say, history—and oh, what a history it was. Wright went on to win multiple NFC Championships and Super Bowls. Decades later, he is still considered to be one of the very best to ever play the offensive tackle position. Today, Rayfield Wright is in the Pro Football Hall of Fame. By the way, so is Tom Landry.

Our Head Coach, our Heavenly Father, can see things in us that we are unable to see in ourselves. The Old Testament prophet Jeremiah declares that God has a plan for each of us that it is good. The plan is full of hope and promises a future. The plan never promises that things would go the way we think they should.

The college we felt we had to attend may not be the place where God intends us to study. The career we worked for years to attain may only be a part of our journey and not our destination. The life goal, which we were convinced we must accomplish, may actually be in the way of achieving something far greater.

How will we respond when our Head Coach summons us with the unwelcome news that we must change positions and put aside our own dreams and aspirations? If we dig in our heels, try to convince ourselves that we misunderstood God, and refuse to follow Him, we can be assured of two outcomes.

First, we will never truly become all that we were created to be; and, we will not experience the joy of being in step with God. But, if like Rayfield Wright, we trust our Head Coach, even when we don't want to, we can be assured of the Victory that is found only in Jesus Christ.

I don't know about you, but I would rather be a Hall of Fame offensive tackle than a bench-warming tight-end any day.

Day *11*

Laughter

He will yet fill your mouth with laughter and your lips with shouts of joy.

(Job 8:21)

Half-Time

We are at the midpoint of our study. Football provides us with a *half-time* so that we can take a break from the game. Why don't we do the same thing? Go ahead, get some Gatorade before you start reading.

Has it ever occurred to you that of all the creatures in the world, we are the only ones with the capacity for laughter? Now, this is not just speculation on my part. I've tested this theory. I've got a Great Dane. And no matter how funny I am (or as some would say how funny I look), I get nothing out of him—not a chuckle, not a grin, not even a smirk. It's true. Animals don't laugh—only people. I really think there's something to this.

I honestly believe laughing is something that God wants us to do. First of all, I don't believe that God would have taken the time to give us the unique ability for laughter if He didn't intend for us to use it. Secondly, the Bible tells us that we are created in the very image of God. So, God laughs too! How awesome is that?! Our God, our great, strong, and powerful God laughs, and He wants us to laugh with Him.

To truly comprehend the joy of Christ, we have to laugh. No, we shouldn't laugh all the time, but I bet many of us are a little bit behind in the laughter department. You see, laughter has the same correlation to joy that walking through the Red Sea had to faith for the Israelites.

Remember the story. Moses and the Israelites had been fleeing from the Egyptian army. They reached the shore of the Red Sea with no place to go. So, Moses prayed and prayed, and God showed off by splitting the sea in half.

What we often forget is that it was pitch dark, and the walls of water had to be louder than we can even imagine. It had to be scary. Nevertheless, there came a time when those folks had to stop praying and start walking.

The same principle is true for us. It's not enough to just claim that we have joy. It's not enough to just say that we trust Jesus. Frankly, it is not sufficient to claim to live by faith and to claim the hope that is Jesus Christ and then just sit there, kind of like my old dog does.

Oh, and by the way, not only is laughter a great outlet for our Christian joy, but it is also very healthy. Physicians tell us that when we laugh, our brains release chemicals called endorphins. These chemicals actually help us fight stress and disease. Is God smart, or what? Many centuries before the medical world came up with a word like endorphin, God said, *"A merry heart does good like a medicine"* (Proverbs 17:22).

The Christian must make laughter a priority. Just as we need air, food, water, and prayer to thrive daily, we also need laughter. And when you laugh, I promise you will bring joy and laughter to those around you, except for Great Danes. Those guys have no sense of humor!

Day *12*

Forgiveness

But when they looked up, they saw that the stone, which was very large, had been rolled away. As they entered the tomb, they saw a young man dressed in a white robe sitting on the right side, and they were alarmed.

"Don't be alarmed," he said. "You are looking for Jesus the Nazarene, who was crucified. He has risen! He is not here. See the place where they laid him. But go, tell his disciples and Peter, 'He is going ahead of you into Galilee. There you will see him, just as he told you.'"

(Mark 16:4-7)

The Interception Matrix

For some reason or another, I have had the "privilege" of coaching several young quarterbacks. Many times in my career, I have started sophomore and even a couple of freshmen quarterbacks. Often, this can be a recipe for disaster. Young quarterbacks make mistakes—a lot of mistakes.

I have learned that how I respond to those youthful mistakes, rather than trying to avoid them altogether, will determine how quickly and smoothly that young quarterback can grow into a confident signal-caller.

Perhaps the most obvious mistake a quarterback can make is to throw an interception. As a coach, I have learned to anticipate these setbacks and prepare my young quarterbacks in advance for the inevitable. I have actually developed an "interception matrix" that I share early and often with young QBs. It may sound silly or over-simplistic, but it works.

Here it is:

You will throw interceptions.

An interception will not kill you or the team.

The sun will come up tomorrow.

I still love you.

Your Mom still loves you.

Jesus still loves you.

You will still be our quarterback.

It is incredibly vital to the psychological health of a fifteen or sixteen-year-old boy to know that his relationship with his coach, or his position on the team, will never be altered because of something he may do wrong.

This is not a football concept but a Biblical one. On the night Jesus was arrested, He told Peter that he would soon deny that he even knew the Lord, not once, but three times. Peter said no way, much like an impulsive teenage boy who can't imagine ever throwing an interception. He was adamant that he would stick by Jesus even if it cost him his life. Of course, Jesus was right and Peter was wrong, and in the next few hours, he lied, not once but three times and denied ever knowing Jesus.

Fast forward three days to the morning Jesus was resurrected. An angel told the women who first saw the empty tomb, *"Go to Galilee and tell the disciples and <u>Peter</u> that Jesus would meet them there."* Why was Peter singled out from the rest of the group? Because Peter was the Lord's quarterback and he had thrown three interceptions.

It was important to Jesus for Peter to know that his failures had not altered their relationship. Peter had been chosen by God to play a special role among the disciples. He truly was the leader or quarterback of the group. Despite Peter's failures, the Head Coach still loved him and had no plans to pull him from the game.

Now here's the really cool thing. Jesus loves you as much as He loved Peter. No matter what you've done or how many times you have messed up, He still loves you. He still has an awesome plan for your life. He wants you in the game, not on the sidelines. He is not worried about interceptions that you threw in the past, and he doesn't want you to be, either.

I go through the "interception matrix" with my quarterbacks because when they make a mistake, we must put it behind us and move on to the next play as fast as possible. Jesus specifically wanted Peter to know he had been forgiven because Peter was in a state of depression, grieving over his own sin. Jesus was ready for Peter to get up and get on with life.

The "interception matrix" only works when young quarterbacks believe it. When they come to the point where they no longer beat themselves up over a bad play, then I know they are ready to go back in the game and play well.

The forgiveness Jesus died to give us only works when we believe it. When we stop torturing ourselves over past failures and accept the fact that Jesus has completely forgiven us, we can enjoy the abundant life He wants for us.

Listen. What's that? I think I hear our Head Coach calling your number. Get back in there!

Day 13

Service

*So He got up from the meal, took off his outer clothing,
and wrapped a towel around his waist. After that, He
poured water into a basin and began to wash his disciples' feet, drying them with the towel that was wrapped
around Him.*

(John 13:4-5)

Super Bowl Scenario

Let me pose a hypothetical question.

Suppose you got a free, 50-yard line ticket to the Super Bowl.
And while we are pretending, let's also suppose that your ticket
came with the opportunity to have a private, one-on-one conversation with absolutely anyone on either team. Who would
you choose?

Would you choose the quarterback? I think a lot of people
would. After all, he is normally the face of the franchise. But
then again, that may be a bit too obvious. Perhaps you would
go off-script. Would it be the head coach? The middle linebacker? The superstar wide receiver?

Of course, I don't know who you would pick. Heck, I'm
not even sure who I would pick. I do think I know who Jesus
would choose. I'm confident that if Jesus had the opportunity to spend quality time with anyone associated with a Super
Bowl team, He would go off-script—way off-script. He would

pick the water-boy.

The water-boy?!! Yep, I think so. Jesus would not be impressed by the athleticism of the players. He would not be awestruck by their speed, size, and strength. He would give no thought to the seven-figure salaries and celebrity status given to pro football players. Instead, He would be enamored with those who serve others. He always has been.

Remember, He told a story about a man from Samaria who went out of his way to help someone in need, even when those from the religious community refused to do so. Remember, He said about Himself that *"The Son of Man did not come to be served but rather to serve others."* Remember that one of the last things Jesus did with His disciples, on the night before He died, was to wash their tired, worn, and dirty feet. He was, and is, the ultimate servant.

We will never experience true victory in this life apart from genuine service to others. It is what we were created to do. It is one of the ways that we, as imperfect humans, can best emulate the perfect Christ. The rewards for service are seldom, if ever, tangible. Notoriety and prestige should never accompany true service—only hard work and self-sacrifice. The benefits of service are all for others—all, that is, but one. The benefit we get to keep when we serve someone else is the euphoric joy of knowing that, in some small way, just for a moment, we were just a little bit like Jesus. It doesn't get any better than that!

Day 14

Prayer

Do not be anxious about anything, but in everything, by prayer and petition, with thanksgiving, present your requests to God. And the peace of God, which transcends all understanding, will guard your hearts and your minds in Christ Jesus.

(Philippians 4:6-7)

Call Time-Out

Time-outs are an interesting part of a football game. To most fans, time-outs are boring. They are an interruption. But to the coach, time-outs are precious. We guard them with our lives and only use them when absolutely necessary. After all, we only get three of them per half.

Coaches know there will be critical moments in the game when we must stop and talk things over with our players. We have to communicate with one another. We have to make sure we are all on the same page. We have a big play ahead, and we need to talk about it.

Here again, football imitates life. Have you ever stopped to think about just how many words we use in a given day? It has to be astronomical, especially in today's world. It seems like we are in a constant race to invent new, better, and faster ways to communicate. We email, we text, we Facebook, we Snapchat, we tweet, we video conference, and every now and then, we even find the time to have an actual, verbal conversation! I bet we easily use tens of thousands of words every day. We talk a lot!

Why? Why has the need for instant communication become so paramount in our lives? Why is personal communication a multi-billion-dollar industry? Because we enjoy it. It's that simple; we like to talk.

I know some of us like it more than others, but for the most part, we enjoy having someone to talk to and being able to communicate with those who are important to us. We've spent the better part of the last two centuries trying to remove the barriers in our communication with others.

The Pony Express riders took letters written to loved ones just as fast as a horse could run. Samuel Morse constructed a code that allowed us to send messages from one end of the country to another. Alexander Bell invented the telephone, and the world changed forever. And today, the means we have to communicate are only limited by our imaginations.

It's funny to think that so much time, effort, and money have been necessary for us to remove the barriers to instant communication. Yet, we've always had the ability to have an instant conversation with God. No wires, no fiber-optics, no handheld devices, no technology ever needed. No matter our circumstances, location, or even our native language, we can talk directly to God.

We call it prayer. I think sometimes that word intimidates us, but it's really nothing more than having a personal conversation with the Lord. It's what we need, and it's what He wants.

In the Gospel of Mark, Jesus and His disciples were entering Jericho, and they met a blind man named Bartimaeus. Now, this guy was in bad shape. He had been blind all of his life. He couldn't work or provide for himself. He survived by eating the crumbs that people would throw at him. When Jesus saw him, He asked the most peculiar and even redundant question:

"What do you want me to do for you?" (Mark 20:51).

Huh? Everybody in Jericho knew what Bartimaeus wanted. I can just hear ol' impulsive Peter whispering to the other disciples, "What's wrong with Jesus? I'm not even the Son of God, and I can tell what this guy needs."

Well, we have to admit, it was kind of strange for Jesus to ask such an obvious question. But, the question was not about what Bartimaeus wanted; it was about what Jesus wanted. You see, Jesus has always wanted a personal, intimate conversation with those He loves. Jesus likes to talk, too. He likes to talk to you.

Conversations with Jesus should be treated just like time-outs. We should think of them as precious. We should not forfeit such an opportunity. We should never make a decision without first calling a time-out and consulting with the only Coach who has never called a bad play.

Jesus wants to hear *your* voice. Isn't that amazing when you stop and think about it? When you call Him, He will take a time-out and give you His undivided attention.

Day *15*

Humility

Do nothing out of selfish ambition or vain conceit, but in humility consider others better than yourselves. Each of you should look not only to your own interest, but also to the interests of others. Your attitude should be the same as that of Christ Jesus.

(Philippians 2:3-5)

Offensive Linemen

The unsung heroes of any championship football team have to be those who play on the offensive line. They have some of the most difficult, strenuous, and essential assignments in all of football, and most of us will never know their names. Great offensive linemen are a rare breed of athlete. They find contentment in doing their job well. At the same time, all of the fame, glamor, and attention is usually given to someone else.

If the quarterback completes a long pass, you can bet offensive linemen were protecting that quarterback from defensive monsters who were trying to devour him. If a running back breaks on a long touchdown run, rest assured an offensive lineman opened the hole for him.

Yet linemen are never given credit for a completed pass or for scoring a touchdown. They don't typically make commercials or hold press conferences. They just play football.

We would do well to adopt the selfless attitude of a great offensive lineman. Because whether we admit it or not, we typically want the credit. We enjoy being the center of attention. We like to be first. The problem with that is that Jesus said, *"The first shall be last and, in order to be truly first, you must make yourself last."* I know it sounds backward, but it is the truth.

As long as my life is focused on me, I will never have victory. I might have momentary excitement, but it will be very short-lived. Self-promotion and hyper self-awareness are never-ending battles. Even if I get the spotlight, I can't keep it. As soon as I build a big house to impress all my friends, one of them will build a bigger one. The moment I get the huge promotion, I'll hear about someone I know making more money than me. It's kind of like buying a new computer today. It's obsolete before you get it out of the box.

Solomon, a brilliant man, said it's like *"chasing after the wind."* (Eccl. 1:17). We are just never going to get there. If we keep trying, we will forfeit our health, our happiness, and our victory in this effort in futility. The only way to really win and find the kind of contentment that will last beyond the latest fad is to put the interests of others ahead of ourselves.

We must be genuinely more concerned about the success, happiness, and well-being of others than we are about our own. This is the only way others can ever see Jesus in us because it is exactly what He did.

The second chapter of Philippians tells us that Jesus humbled Himself and became obedient to death, even the horrible death of the cross. Why would he do that? He actually *was* first. He really *did* have it all. Why would He intentionally give up all of that? It's because He knew that only through His humility could there be hope. Only through His humility could there be peace. His humility, even though it was very painful for Him, literally brought victory to the rest of us.

I've got a feeling that Jesus would be a great offensive lineman.

Day 16

Obedience

*Do not merely listen to the Word, and so deceive your-
selves. Do what it says.*

(James 1:22)

He's the Coach

If you are a football coach or have ever coached, directed,
or led any organization, then you understand that it is often
necessary for others to comply with your decisions without
much, if any, explanation. This is especially true during a football game.

From the time the referee spots the ball and blows his whis-
tle, there are only twenty-five seconds for the coach to determine the play he wants to run, call or signal it in to the quarterback who must tell the rest of team, break the huddle, get
to the line of scrimmage, and snap the ball. Obviously, there
is no time for debate or explanation. Players must do exactly
what the coach prescribes, even when they don't understand
or agree.

Believe it or not, when I was a kid, I didn't always do the right
thing. Who am I kidding? I seldom did the right thing. Because
my mother loved me, she would, as we say in the south, "have
to get on to me." My mother was good at this, and it did not
take long to understand that she was in charge, and I would be
much better off if I would just comply with her instructions.

One of the things that irritated me most during these little bonding sessions with my mom was when I would ask why I was being told no. She would respond with that timeless parental phrase, "Because I said so." I hated to hear that. It was actually worse than being told no in the first place!

To my childish mind, it was as if my mother was trying to keep me from something I wanted to do and had no good reason for it. My youth and self-centeredness prevented me from realizing that there was no other person on Earth who loved or cared for me more than my mom. She always wanted the very best for me and would never tell me anything that she didn't truly believe was in my best interest. She also knew that some things were simply beyond my ability to understand and appreciate. A further explanation would only frustrate me more.

She was teaching me that sometimes we are called to unwanted circumstances, and we must accept them even if we are not privy to the reasons behind them. As I said, my mom was very good at this.

As I've gotten older and hopefully a little wiser, I have really come to appreciate the value in "because I said so." It is a key component that we must accept and even embrace in our relationship with God. He is our ultimate parent and, like any good parent, He only wants the very best for us.

Often, the very best is wrapped up in a big bundle of blind obedience. There are so many examples in Scripture of people who had to obey God simply because He said so, *before* they were able to experience true victory. Abraham, Noah, Moses, Daniel, Joseph, Paul, and many others had to simply say "Yes, sir" and obey God even when the details or justification for their assignments were nowhere to be found.

Unfortunately, the opposite was also true. Remember Adam and Eve? God said, "don't eat that fruit" because He's God and because He said so. That wasn't good enough for them, and look how that turned out!

As we've said many times, God really is the Head Coach of our lives. It is His prerogative to create the game plan and our responsibility to carry it out. The only way to enjoy the real contentment and victory that Jesus died to give us is to first give Him our unconditional obedience—just because He said so!

Day 17

Extraordinarily-Ordinary

*Where is the wise man? Where is the scholar? Where
is the philosopher of this age? Has not God made foolish the wisdom of the world? For since in the wisdom of
God the world through its wisdom did not know him,
God was pleased through the foolishness of what was
preached to save those who believe.*

(1 Corinthians 1:20-21)

Get in the Game

A high school football coach is a lot of things. He's a teacher, an organizer, a paramedic, a surrogate parent, and a part-time psychologist. But of all the roles that a high school coach must play, there is none more important than that of "*Convincer.*"

Yes, I know I just made up a word, but there is no better way to describe what great coaches do all the time. They *convince* their players that they can do something that their own hearts and minds tell them is impossible.

Perhaps this is not as critical in the collegiate and professional ranks, but at the high school level, most kids are all too aware of their own fears and limitations. They read the stats of their opponents. They hear how good the other team is supposed to be, and they believe, at least subconsciously, that they will lose, even before the opening kick-off.

This is when the coach must be the *Convincer*. He has to

make his players believe that they can actually do this. No, we are not as big; no, we don't have as much experience; no, we don't travel in custom buses and wear flashy uniforms as they do; but, we work hard, we have a good game plan, and we have each other. We are just fine being us. We don't need to be like them. We can play. We can win.

I'm afraid we are not much different from many of the high school football players that I have coached. So often, we become convinced that something is missing or incomplete about us. We live with the fear that we are not quite as good as someone else. We believe God will never use us.

Scripture tells us this internal dialogue is simply not true. It is a lie, and it comes straight from Satan. He wants us to think there is nothing special about us and that we have nothing God would want to use to bless others.

The truth is that God has never used the biggest, the best, the magical, or the magnificent to accomplish His tasks. Instead, God has always seemed to select the least obvious, the not so special, the...well...ordinary. Need a few examples? Scripture is full of them.

God needed someone to lead millions of people out of slavery who were being held hostage by the most powerful empire on Earth. So, He chose a guy who had committed murder and made the leaders of that empire so mad that they kicked him completely out of the country. His name was Moses.

Remember the time when Jesus was preaching to thousands of people? It got late, and it was time to eat. The disciples went into panic mode and tried to convince the Lord that there was no way to feed all those people and that He should just send them home. Jesus, however, did not panic.

He looked around for what was already there. He found a boy, a very ordinary boy, who happened to have his lunch with him. It was a very ordinary lunch. No, in this case, it wasn't even good enough to be called ordinary. It was just a few fish and a little bread. It was substandard, to say the least, when you're thinking about feeding thousands of people. But to Jesus, it was perfect. He used that tiny, insignificant amount of food to feed all those people and have plenty left over.

My favorite example of God using what is already there is found in Luke 19:28-35. Jesus tells two of his disciples to go into the city and stop at a particular residence. He said the people there have a young donkey that no one has ever ridden. *"Bring it to Me, and when they ask why, tell them that the Lord needs it."* We can gloss over this story if we're not careful and miss the point.

I've got a feeling that most folks owned a donkey in first-century Jerusalem. It was no big deal. Just as most guys in Texas own a truck, most people back then had a donkey. I'm willing to bet that the man who owned this particular animal never once turned to his wife and said, "Honey, one day, that donkey is going to make us famous!" No. Never happened. This little donkey was just a routine part of life, and it was precisely what the Lord needed.

Think you have nothing that God would ever use? Better look again. Think there is something about you that is too bad, too broken, too ugly, too boring, and too ordinary for God to ever be interested? Better think again. According to His track record, you are the perfect candidate.

Allow the Holy Spirit to be the *Convincer* in your life. Remember, He created you exactly as He wants you. You are ready to play right now. So, get in the game!

———————

Day *18*

The Armor of God

*Finally, be strong in the Lord and His mighty power.
Put on the full armor of God so that you may take your
stand against the devil's schemes. For our struggle is
not against flesh and blood,...but against the powers of
this dark world and spiritual forces of evil. Put on the
full armor of God, so that when the day of evil comes,
you may be able to stand your ground... Stand firm,
with the belt of truth..., the breastplate of righteousness..., and with your feet fitted with the readiness that
comes from the gospel of peace..., take the shield of
faith, the helmet of salvation and the sword of the Spirit,
which is the word of God.*

(Ephesians 6:10-17)

Suit Up

One of the more accurate ways in which football imitates
life is that both are full-contact sports. Neither one is for the
faint of heart. Both will knock you around until you feel that
you can't take it anymore, and then, almost immediately, that
play is over, and it's time to line up and do it all over again.

As a coach for more than 25 years, I would go so far as to
say that it is impossible to go through an entire football season
without experiencing a certain amount of pain. Even on a good
night, when things go well and you win the game, you can be

assured of feeling like you have been hit by a large, mean, and ugly truck when you try to get up the next morning. Anyone who says differently has probably never really played the game.

The same is true with the game of life. Even under the best of circumstances, we will still endure disappointment, temptation, grief, and pain. The idea that Christians are somehow exempt from such natural aspects of life is simply not true. Jesus is perfect, and He was not exempt from the trials of life. He had to endure the worst suffering imaginable! No, if He in His Holiness could not escape the aches and pains of this life, we would be foolish to think that we could.

However, some pain, both on the football field and in life, can and should be avoided. Both contests offer built-in protections that can minimalize, and in some cases even eliminate, a lot of the bumps and bruises. For those protective devices to work, we must apply them. In other words, we've got to suit up!

Thankfully, the technology to keep football players safe has evolved exponentially over the last several years. Protective gear is better today than at any time before. Most of it works extremely well when it is worn correctly. Athletic trainers, physicians, and equipment manufacturers have been able to pinpoint the most vulnerable parts of the body that may possibly sustain an injury while playing football.

The helmet protects the head, brain, and face. Shoulder pads cover large joints as well as provide protection for the heart. Other pads are designed to protect large muscle groups. And don't forget about the shoes. Having the best traction as well as protection for the feet are absolutely essential for the sport of football. It may sound crazy, but a relatively minor injury to the foot, such as turf toe, can sideline a player for weeks or even months.

God provides the same kind of protection for us in the book of Ephesians. Paul is writing to the church, and he tells them they must put on the armor of God. In other words: suit up!

The scripture says that through Jesus, we have access to a helmet that protects the mind and wisdom for decision making. We get that helmet when we accept Jesus as savior. Additionally, God will provide us with protection for the heart, much like a pair of shoulder pads. This breastplate goes on when we diligently practice the righteousness of Christ in our own lives. Paul says even our feet can be prepared and protected for battle when we determine to live in the peace that is Jesus.

Here's the thing about protective gear. You've got to put it on *before* the ball is snapped. Trust me. You don't want to be in the middle of a play, perhaps about to be blindsided by a big, angry linebacker, and suddenly realize that you forgot your helmet!

To emphasize the importance of the helmet and other padding, I have a standing rule for my football players. Once we step on the field, we never take it off. Even when we are practicing and it's time to take a break, you must be on the sideline, completely off the field, before you may slide your helmet off. We believe you play like you practice. So practicing at correctly wearing protective gear makes it second nature when it's game time.

Paul said when we diligently practice applying the full armor of God every day, we will be ready when it's game time. We do not have to fall to the temptation, sin, or whatever spiritual linebacker is trying to sack us. We can withstand the hit— when we suit up!

Day 19

Perseverance

Let us not become weary in doing good, for at the proper time we will reap a harvest if we do not give up.

(Galatians 6:9)

Don't Quit

Who doesn't love a thrilling fourth-quarter comeback? There may be nothing more exciting in sports than watching your team rise from the ashes of defeat and somehow win the game in the final seconds of play. Football lends itself to this type of frenzy. A team can appear to be on life support for the majority of the game and then, all of a sudden, begin to make the plays that ultimately win the game.

Good quarterbacks—I mean, *really* good quarterbacks—understand this aspect of football. Guys like John Elway, Brett Farve, and Peyton Manning were never really out of a game because, regardless of the score or time on the clock, they simply never quit. Growing up in Texas, I had a childhood hero who was one of the all-time best at dramatic, come-from-behind wins.

Roger Staubach, *"Captain Come-Back,"* stole victory from opponents in the final two minutes of a game more than any other Dallas Cowboy in history. Who can forget the infamous *Hail Mary* pass to Drew Pearson that sent the Cowboys to the Super Bowl? I promise the Minnesota Vikings never will!

Staubach's teammates have said that Roger was that rare player who truly never quit. As long as there was any time left on the clock, Staubach genuinely believed he could win. Most of the time, he did.

This is the type of attitude the Bible speaks of in Galatians, chapter six. Actually, it's more than an attitude. It's a way of life. The Christian must live with an uncompromising faith that God is *always* able to achieve victory, regardless of the circumstances. He can win, no matter how much time is left on the clock. He can even win with NO time left on the clock. Just ask Lazarus!

Living a life of perseverance and faith does not come easily or naturally. It is human nature to watch the scoreboard and assume we are too far behind, with too little time, to ever see victory. God would have us ignore logic and human circumstances and focus on His supernatural abilities that are without limits.

So, if you have been praying that a friend or family member would accept Jesus as their savior, but they don't show any interest, keep praying. Don't quit.

If you have been asking God to restore a broken relationship between you and your spouse, but you have not seen any changes yet, keep asking. Don't quit.

If you are trusting God to free you from an addiction or other sin that defeats you, but the truth is you are still struggling, keep trusting. Don't quit.

Live in the knowledge that Jesus has never lost. He will always win! Even on that Friday afternoon, when He died on a cross, and the world assumed the game was over, Jesus was just waiting for the fourth quarter. The fourth quarter came on Sunday morning. Now, that's a comeback!

Day 20

Scripture

All scripture is God-breathed and is useful for teaching, rebuking, correction, and training in righteous, so that the servant of God may be thoroughly equipped for every good work.

(2 Timothy 3:16-17)

Study Your Playbook

Suppose I said to you, "Pro Right Dallas, Z Orbit, 528, Y-Stick?" Confused? What about "Ranger-Gun, Tail Jet, Wham-Boot?" By now, you are probably convinced that at some point, I bumped my head really hard.

Believe it or not, those combinations of gibberish actually provide very specific instructions for my football players. That which, on the surface, appears to make no sense is, instead, a systematic, precise formula that, when understood and followed, allows my team to become very successful. It's part of our playbook.

At the beginning of each football season, all of the players receive a playbook. It is full of diagrams and terminology that initially seem overwhelming. To combat how daunting the entire book can be, we typically concentrate on one or two sections at a time. The players must commit to reading and studying so that the information becomes part of their cognitive memory. Then we go out on the field and actually practice what the book tells us to do.

We do this so much and so often that, before long, that section of the playbook has become second nature to us. Once we do this, something extraordinary occurs. It is more than the players merely learning the playbook. The playbook actually becomes a part of them. It is so ingrained in who they become that when I call a play (which to most people would sound like I'm speaking Klingon), our players can perform at their best, even in very stressful situations.

Our Heavenly Father is our ultimate Head Coach. Fortunately, He loved us enough to provide us with the ultimate playbook, the Holy Bible. It reveals the very nature and personality of God. It chronicles the access we have to a Holy God through the death and resurrection of His Son, Jesus. It provides specific instructions for every situation that we may encounter. Like a playbook, it is a systematic and precise formula for us to experience success and joy. And like a playbook, it can appear to be completely overwhelming.

Ironically, the vastness of the Scriptures is one of the tools used by Satan to keep us from truly experiencing God. So, we must employ some football techniques.

We must commit to reading and studying the Bible in sections. We must repeatedly practice what we study. We must be willing to do more than simply memorize the words on the page. Instead, we must be willing to allow God to truly change us into that which we read about. And just like football practice, we must do this every day!

Of all the different sections in the Bible, there is none greater than the life of Jesus. What an excellent place to start. Begin by studying the Gospels and see for yourself just how amazing Jesus really is.

When we do this, we will have so much more than an academic knowledge of Scripture. It will inspire, lead, and shape us. It will become a part of us. It will allow us to recognize the voice of God and be able to follow Him, love Him, and find our victory in Him, no matter what play He calls!

Day 21

High Expectations

Not that I have already obtained all of this, or have already arrived at my goal, but I press on to take hold of that for which Christ Jesus took hold of me.

(Philippians 3:12)

Win the Game

As I've said before, I believe football to be one of the greatest life illustrations. It has taught me so much, and I am extremely grateful that God has allowed me to be a small part of this great game. My hope has always been that I would use my platform as a football coach to teach young boys the life lessons that will someday aid them in becoming great husbands, fathers, and leaders. I want our time together to have indelible marks on their lives that last beyond their playing days. My prayer, and I believe my responsibility, is to use football to show my players the hope that is Jesus Christ.

Having said all that, let me be clear and candid about something. On Friday nights, when the lights come on, and we hit the field for the opening kick-off, I am not thinking about any of those grander purposes or noble callings. I am concentrating on one objective and one objective only...win the game!

Call me superficial, but I've spent quite a bit of time discussing this with the Lord, and I genuinely believe this is the course He would have me to take. To be the coach God has called me to be, I must, in addition to evangelizing, nurturing, and ministering to our players, instill a commitment and desire to strive for success in every endeavor. I believe scripture teaches that to do otherwise is contrary to the will and nature of God.

Imagine a physician who lives her life according to the principles of the Bible, has a great relationship with Jesus, but is never focused on helping her patients get well. Soon, that doctor would no longer have a practice and no longer have multiple opportunities to share her faith. Imagine an engineer who professes his faith in Christ, and even is bold to share that faith, but who has a track record of building structures that are always substandard and unsafe. What type of Christian witness would that individual be? I would venture to say a not very effective one.

Colossians 3:23 tells us that no matter our job, we should do it with all our hearts as though we are working for the Lord and not for men. Additionally, 2 Corinthians refers explicitly to us as the ambassadors of Christ. These verses remind us of two crucial principles for a championship life.

First, we have a responsibility as Christians to aim for the bar of success that God Himself set for us. He never did anything, from His work during creation to His redemption for us on the cross, which was not His very best effort. His standards are the ones that should matter to us, not those of the world, which often are compromised and apathetic.

The second principle reminds me of a football uniform. A spectator might have a difficult time identifying my football players as individuals during one of our practices. Helmets hide all the faces. Shoulder pads and other gear make all the players look about the same size. Plain, solid-colored practice jerseys are identical from one player to another. Sometimes, even I have to take a second look to tell who is who. But on game night, we dress in very distinct uniforms, different from those of our opponents, and the crowd can easily see which team is ours and who it is that we represent.

When we accept Jesus as our Savior, we put on the uniform of Christianity.

We no longer represent ourselves but Christ, who lives in us. And you can bet the world is watching. Football uniforms are expensive, but they are nothing compared to the price Jesus had to pay for us to be on His team. So, we are honor-bound to strive for success in all that we do and to make sure that we credit God for any success we may enjoy.

So, the Christian employee should strive to be the most productive co-worker at the office. Christian craftsmen should build the finest products. Christian lawyers should attempt to win every case. And Christian football coaches must try to win every game. To accept any less from ourselves compromises our own integrity and weakens the example we set for the God we serve.

Jesus has multiple titles. He is Lord, Savior, healer, counselor, advocate, and so many more that are beyond my comprehension. Ultimately, He is the only undefeated and the greatest Champion the world will ever know. As we play the game of life and do our best to be imitators of Christ, we should always remember that we must play to win!

About the Author

Dr. Cody Moree and his wife, Crickett, make their home in Huntington, Texas. They have two amazing adult children, Chelsi and Chandler.

Cody serves as the Superintendent and Head Football Coach of the Apple Springs Independent School District. He is also a highly sought-after Christian comedian and motivational speaker.

Booking information can be found at www.CoachMoree.com.

Made in the USA
Columbia, SC
07 August 2022

64808567R10040